IMAGES

of America

ROTTERDAM

The coat of arms for Rotterdam was developed in 1952 by the Dutch government, in the Netherlands. It depicts the town's frontier farming roots and industrial present.

On the cover: Four children stand at the edge of the road in front of the Karl family home, located at the corner of Karl and Main Streets in Rotterdam Junction. The picture was taken looking west *c.* 1914.

IMAGES
of America

ROTTERDAM

Schenectady County Historical Society

ARCADIA
PUBLISHING

Published by Arcadia Publishing,
Charleston, South Carolina

Library of Congress Catalog Card Number: 2004107289

For all general information, contact Arcadia Publishing:
Telephone 843-853-2070
Fax 843-853-0044
E-mail sales@arcadiapublishing.com
For customer service and orders:
Toll-free 1-888-313-2665

Visit us on the Internet at www.arcadiapublishing.com

Rotterdam, New York, is a sister city of Rotterdam, the Netherlands.

CONTENTS

The 1866 Beers map shows the location of places in Rotterdam.

INTRODUCTION

Situated near the eastern end of New York State's Heritage Corridor at what is known as the "Gateway to the West," the town of Rotterdam is closely linked with the early development of Schenectady. In 1661, Arent Van Curler from Nykerk, Holland, and 14 other proprietors cleared and settled the area that became the city of Schenectady. At that time the present town of Rotterdam served as the outlying farmlands and wood lots for the settlers. With few exceptions, these settlers made their homes in the Stockade in Schenectady but went to their farmlands during the daytime. One of these exceptions was Elias Van Guysling, who c. 1670 built a house on the Great Flats on the outskirts of the city. This house stood until the late 1940s. Very shortly after Van Guysling had settled, Daniel Janse Van Antwerp applied for a patent of 165 acres of land in the Woestina area, near present-day Rotterdam Junction, and was granted it in 1680. He built the stone house known as the Mabee Farm, which he sold to his business partner Jan Pieterse Mabee in 1705. Arent Bradt, another of the first settlers of Rotterdam, was the grandson of one of the original proprietors of Schenectady. When his father died in 1713, Bradt inherited a piece of property on the Second Flat, and c. 1736, he built the Bradt house, which still stands on Schermerhorn Road. Other families continued to settle the lands now occupied by Rotterdam. Some of the family names include Crawford, Gregg, Pangburn, Putnam, Rynex, Van Eps, Vedder, Veeder, and Wemple. Even so, the area remained a fairly empty wilderness well into the 18th century.

The lands now known as Rotterdam became Schenectady's Third Ward when that city was incorporated in 1798. Rotterdam retained that status when the county of Schenectady was chartered in 1809. During this period, a council of aldermen and assistants from each of the four wards governed the city of Schenectady. The Third Ward, Rotterdam, and the Fourth Ward, Glenville, were the largest wards, but as farming communities they were quite thinly populated. Meanwhile, the city of Schenectady had expanded very rapidly during the Revolution and the period of westward expansion that followed. It became a commercial boatbuilding and trading center. Because of conflicting interests, the farmers from the Third and Fourth Wards seldom agreed with the urban-oriented council members from the other two wards. As a result, in May 1819, the city council recommended that the Third and Fourth Wards be separated out as towns, and on December 31, a petition to the state legislature was drafted. The legislation was passed on April 14, 1820, the final day of the legislative session, creating the town of Rotterdam. In 1821, Peter Becker became the first supervisor and was later returned for two more terms.

As the Erie Canal was being built, between the years 1820 to 1825, towns and villages fortunate enough to be located along the waterway grew and prospered from the trade it spawned. Many of the town's residents were employed as lock tenders and towpath walkers, who checked the structure for leaks, made repairs, and maintained it. There were also those whose shops, hotels, and farms served the canal and profited by it. The Erie Canal ran eight miles through the town along the Mohawk River and the River Road (Route 5S). There were three canal locks in Rotterdam: one opposite the end of Schermerhorn Road, another about one mile farther west, and the third at the end of Lock Street in Rotterdam Junction. *Spaffords Gazetteer* for 1825 listed at that time "2 churches and 7 school houses." The schools were in session eight months of the year, teaching 273 pupils at a cost in public money of $211.50. It also listed the town as having four gristmills, four sawmills, three textile mills, a satin factory, a paper mill, and two "oil" mills. The population was 1,529 and included 29 slaves and 78 free Blacks. Shortly thereafter, the Mohawk and Hudson Railroad, the first line to operate in New York State, was run through Rotterdam lands, crossing today's Hamburg Street at the same point as the modern Penn Central Railroad. In August 1831, when the *Dewitt Clinton* made its maiden run from Albany to Schenectady, many residents were on hand to view what was to bring the greatest economic growth. From this line evolved the great New York Central and later the Penn Central Railroad with the merger of several other short lines between Albany and Buffalo in 1853. In 1866, a single line was run from the town of Athens, up the Hudson River, through Guilderland, to join the New York Central near Hamburg Street in Carman. During 1869, work began on the Schenectady-to-Duanesburg Railroad, which ran out to Quaker Street and connected to the modern Delaware and Hudson, giving access to the coal regions of Pennsylvania. The railroads and the canal prompted the creation of a host of small hamlets within the town of Rotterdam, including Mohawkville, Van Eppsville, Carman, Rotterdam Springs, Pattersonville, South Schenectady, Rotterdam Junction, and Coldbrook. Some of these names are still in use today, and some have faded with the passing of railroads and canals.

During the 19th century, Schenectady County became known as the "Broomcorn Center of the World," for more broomcorn was raised and more brooms and brushes were made in this county than in any other area of the world. Broomcorn, resembling maize but without ears, grows especially well in rich fertile soil; so, the flat alluvial areas near the Mohawk River were ideal. The 10-mile strip of land along the river from the city of Schenectady to Pattersonville consisted almost exclusively of farms producing corn and brooms. The industry drove the economy of Rotterdam from c. 1835 until the introduction of cheaper western corn in the 1880s wiped out the thriving industry and the local farmers switched to more profitable dairy farming or shifted to the newly blossoming industrial plants of Schenectady.

By World War I, many of Rotterdam's residents worked in the large industrial complexes of the General Electric Company and the American Locomotive Company in Schenectady or in supporting areas like the Army Supply Depot, off Curry Road. After World War II, much of Rotterdam was transformed, as many of the old estates and farms were subdivided into developments with low-cost, mass-produced housing. A new slogan, "The Town of Tomorrow," promoted Rotterdam as a place of "good schools, good neighbors, and good living."

Through three centuries, Rotterdam has changed, developed, and prospered. From a strictly rural beginning, Rotterdam has responded to the needs of the times through industrialization, war, and suburbanization. Yet, evidence of its earlier history remains. The Mabee Farm Historic Site and the old locks of the Erie Canal are two living history sites. "Stronger Through Effort" is the challenging motto on Rotterdam's town seal, and the efforts undertaken today will move the town forward to discover new roles for the 21st century.

One

ROTTERDAM

Adam Vrooman built a mill on the Sandkill in 1683. In 1690, when Schenectady was destroyed, he saved his own life by brave conduct in defending his house. His first wife and infant child, however, were killed. His two sons, Wouter and Barent, were taken as prisoners to Canada. In 1697, Vrooman went to Canada to obtain their release. On their return, the two sons purchased land west of Schenectady. In the background is the Watson Vrooman Farm.

The Vedder House was built in the middle of the 18th century. The picture was taken in 1953, just before the house was torn down to make way for Exit 26 of the New York State Thruway.

Harmen Albertse Vedder was among the early proprietors in Schenectady; he received patents in 1664 and 1667. His son Arent had a house on Washington Avenue in Schenectady and farms at Hoffman's and the "Woestyne." In his 1755 will, Arent Vedder left this farm to his son Symon. Pictured are the front hall and the staircase.

The Van Slyke House is located on River Road (Route 5S). It is more than 150 years old and boasts eight fireplaces. The Van Slyke family came to the area in 1634.

In 1973, Exit 26 of the New York State Thruway was changed to provide access to a proposed bridge to Scotia. The bridge was completed in 1999.

The unused and dry Erie Canal and towpath are shown before the canal was filled in. This picture was taken near Exit 26 of the New York State Thruway.

The Major Crounse House, on Schermerhorn Road, is shown in the foreground. The Bradt House and the Schermerhorn Mansion are on the right. The Crounse House was moved when Route 890 was constructed. The picture dates from November 23, 1952.

Arent Samuelse Bradt and Catrina Mabee constructed the Bradt House on Schermerhorn Road
c. 1736. Bradt was 10 years old at the time of the Schenectady Massacre of 1690. He survived,
but his parents did not. The lower view shows the home with side additions.

Arent Bradt was a brewer by trade. He was a trustee of the common lands of Schenectady and a member of the New York Provincial Assembly of 1745. This is a closeup of the Bradt House.

In 1934, Vincent Schaefer photographed the Schermerhorn Mansion, on the right, and the Bradt House. Among the trees is the Schermerhorn Dutch Barn. In the center distance is the feeder canal for the Edward Yates Gristmill.

Jacob Schermerhorn built the Schermerhorn Homestead in 1757. The frame wing was added in 1796. This is the second Schermerhorn house; the other one is known as the Schermerhorn Mansion.

In 1701, Johannes Teller built the Teller-Schermerhorn Barn after his return from Canada, where he had been held prisoner after the Schenectady Massacre. His daughter Margarita married Jacob Schermerhorn. In 1948, Vincent Schaefer acquired the barn and dismantled it. While removing the building, he researched Dutch barn construction and learned how architecturally and historically important these buildings were. The experience led him to create the Dutch Barn Preservation Society.

This photograph, taken from the Glenville Hills in the 1940s, shows Yantaputchaberg (now called Crawford Mountain). Visible in the background is the Hoffman's Cutoff, the connection for the West Shore and the old New York Central Railroads.

Yantaputchaberg is shown from the mouth of the Plotterkill. Vincent Schaefer, who formed the Mohawk Hiking Club, took the picture in 1934. Schaefer was a General Electric engineer who was most famous for creating artificial rain by cloud seeding. He lived on Schermerhorn Road.

Plotterkill is derived from the Dutch words *Platte* (flat) and *Kill* (creek). With its source near Rynex Corners, the Plotterkill descends 900 feet to the Mohawk River. In 1978, it was purchased and placed under the charge of the Schenectady County Nature and Historic Preserves.

Unidentified people visit the Plotterkill Falls in the early spring, possibly for a picnic. The picture was taken c. 1890.

W. C. Vrooman photographed the Plotterkill Creek on September 21, 1890. His friend William H. Peckham holds the photo case. Peckham was part owner of Peckham and Van Vorst, a lumberyard in Schenectady.

The Ground Observer Corps meets at Airplane Observation Post 21B. Theodore Mabee is the bugler, and Herbert J. Terry, on the left, is in charge. The others are unidentified.

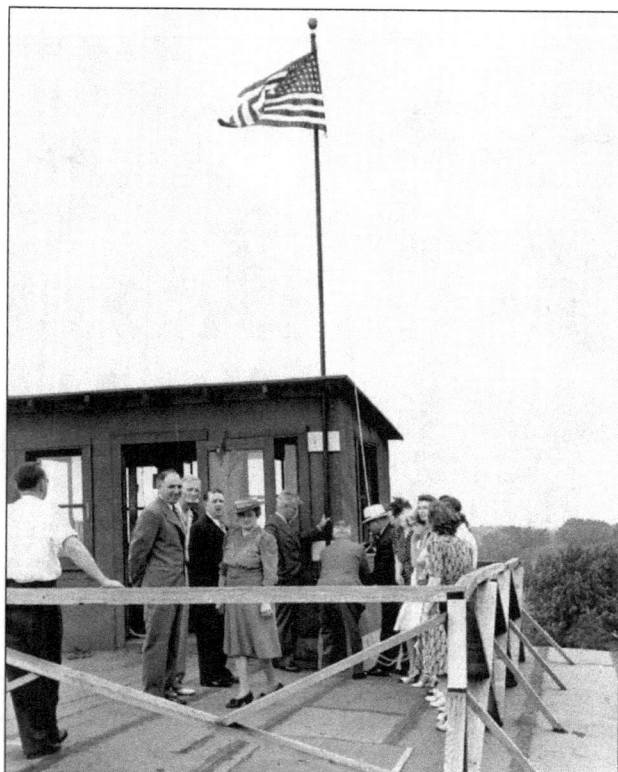

A flag ceremony is held in the 1940s at Airplane Observation Post 21B, on top of one of the Rotterdam Hills. The purpose of the corps was to identify planes flying overhead during World War II.

Enlargement of the U.S. Army Depot began in 1918 during World War I. Originally, it opened during the Civil War as the Army Storage Depot.

This December 10, 1918, photograph shows construction at the U.S. Army Depot. The garrison is visible in the background.

The Siegel Farm, located on Olean Street, served as a campground for the 27th Division of the U.S. Infantry in 1918.

In 1918, the division was called to serve in World War I in France. The 27th Division marches in formation.

The troops are shown in the review parade on their way to the railroad station.

The troops are aboard the railroad Pullmans, ready to travel to New York City and then embark for France during World War I.

WINDSOR CASTLE.

Soldiers of the United States, the people of the British Isles welcome you on your way to take your stand beside the Armies of many Nations now fighting in the Old World the great battle for human freedom.

The Allies will gain new heart & spirit in your company.

I wish that I could shake the hand of each one of you & bid you God speed on your mission.

George R. I.

April 1918.

Each soldier received the following letter from Windsor Castle: "Soldiers of the United States, the people of the British Isles welcome you on your way to take your stand beside the Armies of many Nations now fighting in the Old World the great battle for human freedom. The Allies will gain new heart & spirit in your company. I wish that I could shake the hand of each one of you & bid you God speed in your mission. George R. I. April 1918."

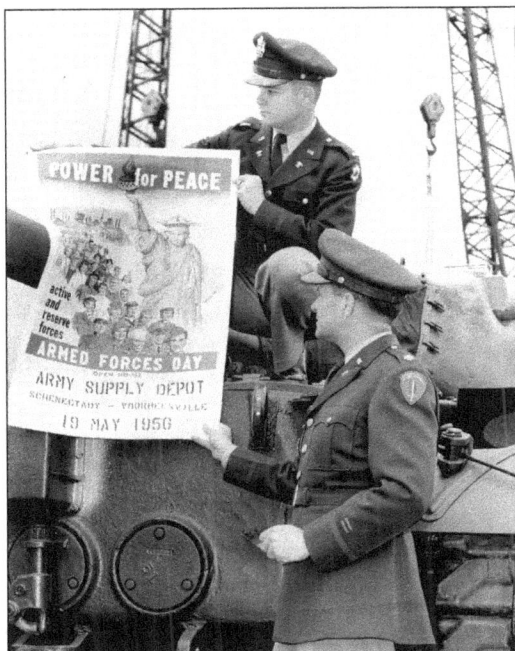

Lt. Col. R. W. Burk (standing) and Lt. Ray Smith examine a poster for an open house. They are on an M-47 tank at the Schenectady Army Depot on May 7, 1956.

A large boulder taken from Waverly Place in Schenectady was located at the northwest corner of Rice Road and Washington Avenue near the General Electric Company. Estimated to have weighed between 14 and 20 tons, the boulder was dedicated to Edwin Wilber Rice Jr., a great pioneer of the electrical industry. It was erected by the city on June 12, 1936, to mark the electrical industry's 50th anniversary in Schenectady. Pictured are H. L. Reed (left) and Chester J. Woodin from the Schenectady County Historical Society. The plaque was given to the historical society when the New York State Thruway spur was constructed in 1965. The boulder was destroyed.

Artesian wells are very deep wells of pressurized water compressed between layers of rock. In this 1894 photograph, men under the direction of Richard Walton are testing the wells for flow before building the pump station.

Schenectady's artesian water wells were dug between 1894 and 1897. The pumping station was located on Old River Road in Rotterdam.

Shown is the interior of the pumping station *c.* 1896. Water was pressurized by the use of coal-fired steam pumps.

Mr. and Mrs. Sarcher Smith relax on the porch. Smith, a big, powerful man, always went to cockfights in Canada with Col. Daniel David Campbell. If a fracas started, Smith picked the battlers up bodily and threw them out. He toted flour barrels as an employee of the Carley Brothers Feed Store, on State Street in Schenectady.

Col. Daniel David Campbell built Two-Mile House. It was better known as Maser's Bull's Head Tavern, a name it took from Adam Maser, the butcher who ran the hotel. A large sign with a bull's head hung from the building. The inn burned in 1888 and was replaced by a three-story building known simply as Two-Mile House. It was located two miles from Schenectady.

A familiar landmark in the area, the new Two-Mile House was famous for gala events. The tavern catered to cockfights, illicit gambling, dances, and varied celebrations.

Lock 23 of the Erie Canal was known as Alexander's Lock. Built in the 1840–1841 expansion of the Erie Canal, it was double chambered and made of limestone. Lock 23 was used to raise and lower boats eight feet. A total of 38,344 lockages occurred in 1850. Alexander's Lock was extended in the 1889–1890 reconstruction of the canal. Traveling the canal by boat was a popular Sunday afternoon pastime.

In the background are the Erie Canal and Mount Yantaputchaberg. The oxbow of the Mohawk River and the island disappeared when the Barge Canal was built in 1918. The Barge Canal replaced the Erie Canal and used the Mohawk River.

In the foreground are tracks for the newly engineered electric streetcars, a joint project between the General Electric Company and the Schenectady Railway Company. The crowds nearby are believed to be observing a test. To the left is an electric mule pulling a pair of canal boats along the Erie Canal.

The electric mule was used to replace mules on the canal. This track ran from the General Electric Company west. The closeup of the electric mules shows the cable that was used to connect the barge to the mule. Company buildings are on the left.

In the background are the General Electric Company (left) and the Gilbert Car Works. The broomcorn fields produced broomcorn until the 1890s, when the General Electric Company took over the land and developed Edison Park. The land later became the site of more factories.

Men make railroad cars and streetcars inside the Gilbert Car Works. Notice the use of wood.

Van Eppsville was located on the Mohawk River at the foot of the Campbell Avenue Bluff on the west side of the present General Electric Company. In the 1840s, there was a family-owned business complex operated by J. and A. Van Eps. Together, they ran a broom factory, a broadcloth factory, and a flour mill.

In 1924, on the Rotterdam Flats, the General Electric Company constructed a great transmitter laboratory for the development of radio. It consisted of one large, one-story brick structure and numerous framed structures, each with its transmitter and related apparatus. The antenna structures consisted of three 300-foot steel towers and one 150-foot tower.

Construction of the second Western Gateway Bridge began in 1923. This bridge replaced the Mohawk Bridge, which connected Scotia and Schenectady. The first Western Gateway Bridge opened in 1916 in Rotterdam Junction.

Forms are being poured for the construction of the Western Gateway Bridge's many arches. The bridge was built mostly of concrete.

Arch No. 24 collapsed on September 17, 1923. Four men were killed in the accident, and 450 tons of concrete landed in the Mohawk River.

Dedication of the bridge took place on June 11, 1926, with Gov. Alfred E. Smith attending. Some 75,000 people came to the program and 10,000 cars were parked nearby. A parade ensued with 2,000 marchers.

34

The completed second Western Gateway Bridge is shown here with its famous "Dead-man's Curve" and sodium lights. Sodium lights were a recent development and were the first lights to illuminate highways.

The third Western Gateway Bridge was built in 1974. Demolition of the 1925 bridge occurred after completion of the new bridge. The eastern approach is in the city of Schenectady, and the western approach is in Scotia. The center of the bridge is in Rotterdam.

Elias Van Guysling built the Van Guysling House *c.* 1670. He was a survivor of the Schenectady Massacre. The house was torn down in the 1940s and replaced by General Electric's Turbine Building (Building 273).

Tippecanoe was on Princetown Road on land once owned by the Schermerhorns. Springs fed the Poentic Kill, which ran through the area. The stream was dammed, and a swimming hole was formed. The water was extremely cold and the terrain around the pond rough, as seen in this 1930s photograph. In 1943, the YMCA acquired Camp Tippecanoe and ran it as a day camp and a boarding camp for boys.

The Daniel David Campbell Mansion, built in 1832, was located where Rotterdam Square Mall is today. It was the first residence in Schenectady to have a telephone, which was connected to the police department.

The Campbell coach, shown here in a 1898 parade marking the 100th anniversary of Schenectady's charter, was sold in the 1920s to the Henry Ford Museum in Detroit for $1,700.

The Campbell Sawmill was located on Burdeck Street near present Route 159. The sawmill was not far from the Campbell Mansion. John D. Campbell's two sons operated it.

Refrigerator tool workers from the General Electric Company pose for a picture at Campbell Park (part of Hillhurst Park) in the 1930s. Various General Electric departments often picnicked here.

Weber Electric Company was on the corner of Olean Street and West Campbell Road, now occupied by Old Brick Furniture Store. The company made porcelain light fixtures and various household electrical goods. A porcelain factory was located nearby, about where the Rotterdam fireman's training facility stands today.

The Rotterdam Fire Training Center was built in 1970 on Burdeck Street. It is a place to practice rescue operations. The complex contains a two-story house, a tower, classrooms, an oil tanker truck body, a 2,000-gallon drafting tank, and transformers for simulating electrical fires.

The Second Reformed Church of Rotterdam was built in 1822. This building, at the corner of Putnam Street and Princetown Road, was demolished in 1895, when the present Cobblestone Church was built.

Bradford Gilbert, an architect from New York City, designed the Cobblestone Church in 1895. The architect contributed $800 for the clock tower. The clock was from a New York Central Railroad Station.

The first Draper School was built in the early 1900s on Guilderland Avenue Extension not far from the four corners of Guilderland Avenue and Curry Road. It was named for Andrew S. Draper, a commissioner of education. It burned on May 14, 1914.

A new Draper School was built on Mill Lane (now Draper Avenue) in 1913. In 1920, the high school was added. Draper School was a Union Free School District until Mohonasen School District absorbed it during the 1986–1987 school year.

Jefferson School (District 11) was constructed after World War II. It became part of Schalmont Central School District in 1955. Teacher Constance Flood (back right) poses with her class of fifth-graders in 1961. From left to right are the following: (first row) Joseph Lomonaco, Robert Smith, Stanley Kwiatkowski, Steven O'Brien, and Alan Burk; (second row) Kathy Van Wormer, Suzette Plant, Sharon Rybij, Leah Pendergast, Denise Conklin, Nina Lockwood, and Joanne Sierocki; (third row) Stephen Newton, Cindy Weisheit, Sharon Matula, Deborah Rockwell, Sandra Leschen, and JoAnn Hotaling; (fourth row) Theodore Evenden, Larry Mudrey, Eric Eichler, James Andrews, Daniel Kelly, Gary Feuz, William Ness, and Richard Conrad.

The 1949 Schonowe School kindergarten class is shown here playing. The school is located near the corner of Putnam and Schermerhorn Roads. It also became a part of the Schalmont Central School District.

This picture of a group from the Gregg Road School was taken in the springtime *c.* 1906.

This is Rotterdam School No. 8, also known as the Edgewood School, as it appeared in 1925. It was located at the intersection of Altamont Avenue and Curry Road, now the site of Malozzi's Restaurant. John Bigsbee was the principal of this school.

The Bigsbee School was built on land occupied by Rotterdam School No. 8. The last year the school was used was 1977. It was torn down in 1988 to build Malozzi's Restaurant.

Putman School (Rotterdam District 6) was located on the present Putnam Road. It was the last one-room schoolhouse in Rotterdam. The last classes were held in 1953, with 24 children in the class.

The Mohawkville School was built in 1375 at the end of Crane Street at Altamont Avenue. In 1922, it was equipped as an open-air school for children who had tuberculosis. It was torn down shortly afterward.

Three of the seven Vrooman brothers—Walter, Dewey, and Foster—pose for a picture in 1905.

James Fisher founded the Fisher Methodist Church on August 15, 1849. It was a one-man congregation, since he was the preacher, sexton, organist, choir, and congregation. In 1950–1951, the church was moved from its site on Helderberg Avenue to its present location on Curry Road. Between 1961 and 1963, the church was razed and a new sanctuary (below) was built over the old foundation.

The William Van Dyke House was built in 1847. It is a brick-lined house and is located on Helderberg Avenue. It is one of the few old homes remaining in this area due to development.

The Trinity Reformed Church, built in 1962, is located on the corner of Westcott Avenue and Curry Road. On March 27, 1931, the Mizpah Reformed Church and the Baracah Tabernacle Church merged to form Trinity Reformed Church.

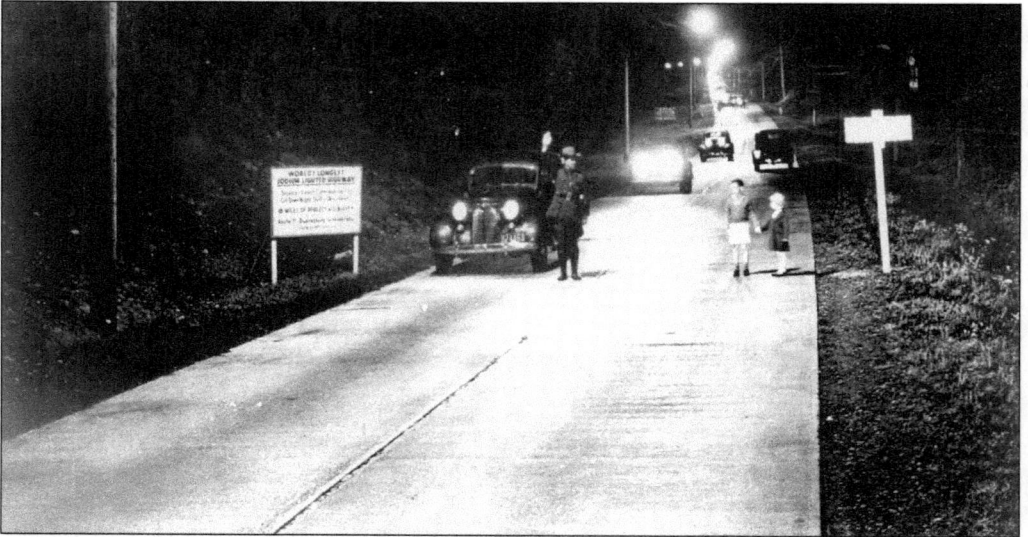

Route 7 was the world's longest sodium-lighted highway before World War II, extending 18 miles from Duanesburg to Schenectady. The General Electric Company made these lights, which were said to cut down on nighttime traffic accidents and required little maintenance. Prior to this time, roads were unlit.

The Myers House was located near Van Eppsville. It was taken down when the Delaware and Hudson Railroad north track was built. Pictured here is a family gathering of three generations. In the left foreground are Charles Galling, Andrew Vogel (an actor), and James Smith. In the back are Grandfather Sauter, Grandmother Sauter, and Charlie Myers. Standing on the porch are Miss Hilburt, Ed Sauter, Miss Hilburt from Buffalo, Mother Myers, Aunt Mary Mayer, Charles Sauter, and George Mayer (with the top hat). The children are N. I., J. C., Will Myers, and Baby Mayer with Miss Smith beside her. In the center foreground are Wealey Sauter, Garry Myers, and an unidentified girl.

Poutre Pond, also known as Putnam Pond for a previous owner, was a local swimming hole with a diving board and bathhouse. It belonged to Joseph Poutre. It is shown here on May 16, 1950.

In 1952, Poutre Pond was filled in to become Rotterdam Memorial Park baseball field, bordered by South Broadway, Westcott Road, and Curry Road.

On the left is the Blue Ridge Service Station, run by Ken Koulter. On the right is the Mobil Station, owned by Clarence King. The two gas stations were located on Broadway near Poutre Pond and were photographed in 1938.

Our Lady of Assumption was originally a mission church of Our Lady of Mount Carmel in Schenectady. Its purpose was to meet the needs of the Italian-speaking community in Rotterdam. The mission lasted from 1924 to 1932, when it became independent. In 1963, the new church was built on Princetown Road and Ford Avenue.

The Dellemont-Wemple House is located on Wemple Road off Dunnsville Road. Hendrick Dellemont built it c. 1790. His son Jacob Dellemont inherited the farm c. 1820.

The Dellemont-Wemple Barn was built c. 1770. The farm is a part of a 1714 patent issued to Arent Van Patten, Mindert Schuyler, and John Dellemont. John Wemple enrolled in the 2nd Albany County Militia in 1775. He married Maria Swits, and their son, Gerritt Wemple, married Nancy Dellemont.

At approximately 7:23 p.m. on Friday, June 24, 1960, a violent twister, of tornado-like velocity, ripped a three-mile path of destruction through Rotterdam, Schenectady, and Niskayuna. It struck the western part of Rotterdam first, following a direction westerly through Carman, Woodlawn, and Niskayuna.

At least a dozen homes were destroyed, scores of others were heavily damaged, and thousands of residences were without electricity or telephone service for a number of days.

From 1890 to 1920, the John Gifford family occupied this house on the Gifford Farm. The house later became known as the Tenant House.

The Gifford Farm, located on Mariaville Road near Rynex Corners, is shown c. 1893. From left to right are Andrew Gifford, an unidentified person, Mary Wingate Gifford, Nettie Gifford, Henry Gifford, and John Gifford. Andrew Gifford lived on the farm from 1920 to 1940.

James Gregg operated the saloon across the road from the post office at Rynex Corners. The team driver is unidentified. The little girl is probably Leah Gregg. The building was removed in the 1930s.

Delmet Gregg ran the store and post office c. 1880. Rynex Corners at that time was large enough to have a cheese factory, grocery store, tavern, and post office.

G. P. Conde's House is pictured above. George P. Conde was a prominent farmer in the area. He married Isabella Ostrom.

Members of Rotterdam Kiwanis prepare for a benefit auction in the early 1950s.

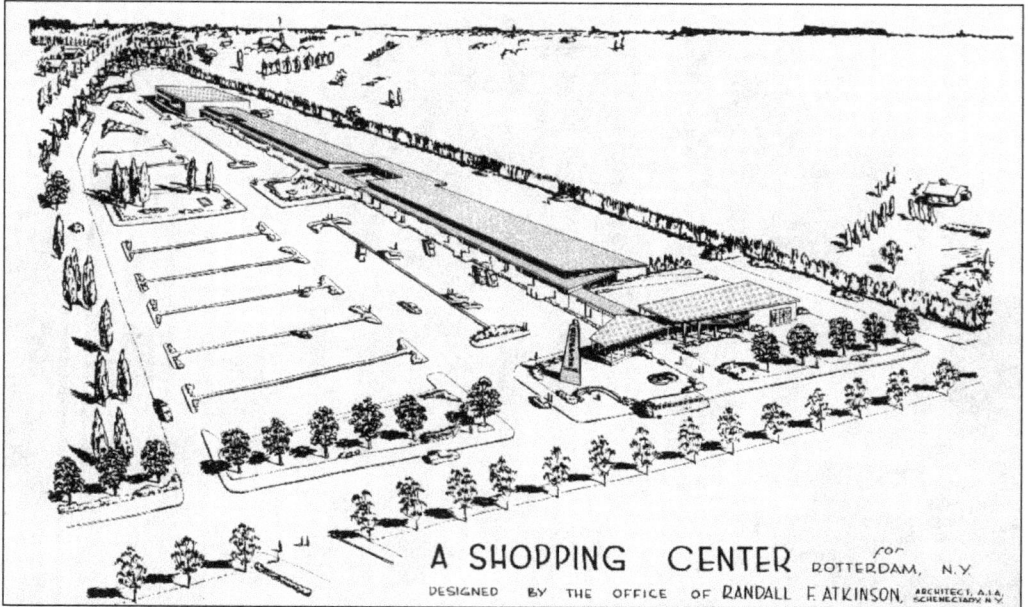

This is an artist's sketch of the proposed $750,000 Shoperama, on Altamont Avenue and Patton Drive. The shopping center containing 14 to 16 stores was completed in 1955. It was the first mall in Rotterdam. Woolworth's and the Grand Union were the anchor stores. Later, Carl's Department Store was added to the mall.

Curry Road Shopping Center was constructed shortly after Shoperama, but its life span was much shorter. Grant's department store closed in the early 1960s, and the Price Chopper grocery store moved to Altamont Avenue shortly thereafter. Space was available to rent, as shown on the sign, but traffic congestion in the area may have contributed to the plaza's closing.

More and more stores left Curry Road Shopping Center. Eventually, the windows were boarded up. For decades, the plaza has stood empty.

The Republican Club, located between Thompson Street and Burdett Road, has been the scene of many picnics held by various organizations. A large ball field is behind the buildings. The facility was well used from the 1950s to the 1980s. It is currently for sale.

Vedder Family Cemetery

This historic burial plot contains the remains of descendants of Harmen Albertse Vedder, an original settler of Schenectady.

He purchased the land and built a home in 1672.

Harmen died around 1715 and is probably buried here.

After purchasing this site from Harmen's great-grandson, Johannes Vedder, Colonel Daniel David Schermerhorn Campbell replaced the home with a 26-room mansion in 1832.

The Vedder family cemetery is in the parking lot of Rotterdam Square Mall. The mall was built in the 1980s amid much controversy over an aquifer and the historical significance of the area.

This picture shows how close to one of the mall entrances the cemetery is located. The contract with the mall states that the cemetery must be maintained.

Two

ROTTERDAM JUNCTION

In 1883, the West Shore Railroad began construction of a rail yard that was completed in 1884. The line was later leased by the New York Central Railroad. Also in 1883, the Fitchburg Railroad was built. The Fitchburg and the West Shore Railroads intersected at Rotterdam Junction. Pictured in front of the Rotterdam Junction Freight House are W. L. McDonald, C. F. Mather, G. A. Kent, C. Eldridge, and B. Butler.

The roundhouse and turntable were located in Rotterdam Junction. Minor engine repairs, maintenance, and emergency repairs were done here. The roundhouse was adjacent to the Mabee House Hotel. Standing on the engine, third from the right, is James Franklin Phillips.

The Fitchburg Railroad grain elevator, which burned in 1918, could hold 484,000 bushels of grain. In 1890, the Boston and Maine Railroad absorbed the Fitchburg Railroad. Thereafter, the New York Central and the Boston and Maine Railroads serviced Rotterdam Junction.

The house known as the Turnbull-Veeder House dates from the late 18th century. It is located west of the Woestina Reformed Church on Route 5S.

Houses along Putnam Street are shown in a picture taken c. 1900.

The second-oldest farm in Rotterdam Junction originally belonged to the Bradts. The family grew broomcorn on the farm. In the 20th century, the Endries family and, later, Everett Candages ran the place as a dairy farm and gave pony rides to children. The Keepers of the Circle, a Native American organization, now leases the land from Schenectady County.

This 1940s picture shows Cartwright's Store, which had been recently renovated. An overhang and a new addition were added. In front of the building are new Texaco gas pumps. The building was located just east of Woestina High School.

The *Kittie West* was built on Oneida Lake near Sylvan Beach in the 1880s and was sold to Schenectadians John N. Parker, Edgar D. Joyner, and James L Foote. It was bought principally for local traffic between Schenectady and Rexford, the local summer resort. Passenger rates to Rexford were 15¢ one way and 25¢ round trip. After 25 years of service, the *Kittie West*, then carrying freight, ran aground and was burned near St. Johnsville.

The *Kittie West* excursion boat is seen near Crawford Road in Rotterdam Junction. Rotterdam Springs Hotel (background) was owned by a Mr. O'Loughlin. The sign advertizes a department store in Schenectady.

The Rotterdam Springs Hotel not only overlooked the Erie Canal but also fronted on Crawford Road. Rotterdam Springs became Lower Rotterdam Junction.

A large barge in the early 1900s has just made its way through Lock 25 of the Erie Canal in Rotterdam Junction. The Erie Canal closed to traffic in 1918. It was replaced by the New York State Barge Canal, which used the Mohawk River.

Scrafford's Store adjoined the Mabee House Hotel on Main Street. George Scrafford (center) and his wife, Rachel Mabee Scrafford, owned both. They built the hotel, which was the first in Rotterdam Junction to accommodate the workers who were building the rail yards. William Kerns (left) was the hotel bartender. The Scrafford's daughter, Mabel (center distance), took over the Mabee estate in 1922, after the death of her parents.

George Scrafford (in the white apron) stands in front of the Mabee House Hotel and Scrafford Store.

This view was taken looking down Main Street *c.* 1910. The Mabee House Hotel is on the left, and the post office and the Hake and Marlette Store are on the right.

Shown is Main Street at the corner of North Street (now Lock Street) *c.* 1902. The building on the right was originally the Independent Order of Odd Fellows (IOOF) building. It is now an apartment house. District No. 5 School is on the left.

The Pattersonville-Rotterdam-Schenectady Transportation Company bus line provided a way for people to travel between the towns From left to right are Sam Putman, Ed Huff, Nettie Vedder, Emma Pitney, Bessie, Mrs. Huff. Helen Van O'Linda, Mrs. Ed Van O'Linda, Harv Van O'Linda, Anna Louise Philips, and Ruth Philips. The picture was taken c. 1910.

An accident occurred on the Route 5S bridge over the Erie Canal c. 1915. George A. Welcome ran the bus company. Mayor J. Teller Schoolcraft and his family were in the car on the road behind the bus and were the first on the scene to help with the rescue effort.

Beyond the excavation is the Candage's Dairy Farm. The land originally belonged to the Bradt family.

A train wreck occurred on the black bridge that crosses Route 5S between Rotterdam Junction and Pattersonville in the fall of 1946. The train was on its way to connect with the West Shore Railroad line. Tony Casso and Jack Pistolesties worked on the wreck.

Construction of the bridge over Lock 9 took place in 1915–1916. When the bridge opened on July 15, 1916, it was referred to as the first Western Gateway Bridge.

This is an aerial view of the completed first Western Gateway Bridge. It also shows Lock 9 of the Barge Canal.

Shown is a program for the opening of the first Western Gateway Bridge.

Jud Dennison is driving the float in the parade marking the opening of the first Western Gateway Bridge, which is Route 103.

This is the original First Reformed Church of Rotterdam (Woestina Church). It was organized in 1784 at Hoffman's Ferry (Vedder's Ferry). The building was moved across the ice on the Mohawk River from West Glenville to this location in the 19th century. It burned on November 9, 1935.

The new church was fashioned after the original and was dedicated in 1936. Metropolitan Opera singer Olive Kline Houlihan soloed at the church. Her maternal ancestors were from Dorn Road in Pattersonville.

Miss Brown accompanied the Rotterdam Junction Methodist Church Sunday school class. The Methodist church was originally located on the Mabee Farm. It was built in 1896 and was moved to its present location c. 1906.

St. Margaret of Cortona was the Roman Catholic church in the town. The picture shows a first communion class on the front steps of the church c. 1929. In 2004, the church celebrated its 100th anniversary.

District No. 5 School stood on the corner of Main and School (later Bradt) Streets. The school, at 1264 Main Street, is now the home of Mechanical Management Inc.

District No. 5 School (Woestina), pictured in 1902, was the only school district with a complete kindergarten-through-12th-grade program. The school was built on a single level in the late 1800s and was later raised and placed atop a new first floor.

Woestina School opened in 1916 as a high school. The lower grades were added in 1920. After consolidation with Schalmont Central School District, Woestina remained a kindergarten-through-eighth-grade school.

The Pattersonville Telephone Company was founded in 1902. Telephone poles were purchased from the Schenectady Illuminating Company on February 28, 1908, and John Ennis and Isaac Frank Patterson of Pattersonville strung the first wires for the company. For the first four decades, the telephone office was housed in various homes, the last one being the McDougall home, which had the first telephone in town, for a cost of $1 a month. In 1942, the independent telephone company moved into its own building, on the corner of Route 5S and Route 103 in Rotterdam Junction, where it still operates today.

Will Turnbull and Lily Schermerhorn, descendants of early Rotterdam settlers, relax in their yard in the late 1920s. This home is still standing on the corner of Route 5S and Turnbull Lane.

This Red Cross Unit was active during World War I. Among the members pictured are Carnie Baker, Mrs. Daniels, Pearl Dowling, Mrs. Orton, and Mrs. Willey.

This tavern on Route 5S dates from the middle of the 19th century. It was a part of Rotterdam Springs that became known as Lower Rotterdam Junction. It served Lock 25 as a farm-to-canal transfer point.

Three

PATTERSONVILLE

Dockstader's Store was located on Route 160 in Pattersonville. E. E. Dockstader operated the store at the foot of Doug Hill in 1900; before that, A. J. Kline sold groceries from the same store in 1895. A delivery wagon from Amsterdam sits in front of the store.

This is an aerial view of Pattersonville, showing Route 5S, the main road through the center of the town, and the West Shore Railroad tracks. The road coming in from the left in the lower left is Rynex Road, on which the fire station and Hudson food store were located. Route 160 comes in from the left near a group of buildings that include the Dockstader store and creamery.

The West Shore Railroad Station was located in Pattersonville. The West Shore and the Boston and Maine Railroads flourished c. 1900. The boom continued until the hump for switching freight cars was opened in Mechanicville.

Members of the West Shore maintenance crew take time to pose for a picture. Identified are Emmet Smith, second from the left, and Carl Struensee, fourth from the left. The Jeffers house is on the right.

A milk truck was hit by a train at the freight station c. 1935.

Dr. Alexander Ennis, a physician and surgeon, resided on Florida Road in Pattersonville. A charge for a home visit ranged from 25¢ to $2.50. In 1885, Ennis's collections amounted to $1,471. He treated many illnesses, among them, typhoid fever, croup, and impetigo. His medications included cod liver oil, witch hazel, and iodine. At a meeting of physicians held in the Ennis home in the late 1800s, it was decided that the best treatment for acute appendicitis was laxatives. Today, that is thought to be a lethal treatment.

This photograph of Rynex Corners was taken from the knoll west of the Gifford Barn *c.* 1880. The cheese factory and the blacksmith shop are on the right. The families of the area at the time were Bradshaw, Bradt, Rynex, Schermerhorn, Gregg, and Turnbull.

Schooling in Pattersonville in the early 1900s centered around Princetown District 6 schoolhouse, located on Florida Road. This school served children from both Princetown (another town in Schenectady County) and Pattersonville. Known as the Pine Grove School, it had classes for students from first grade to eighth grade. In the 1920s, it burned. A new Pine Grove School was constructed, and in the consolidation of the 1950s, it became a part of the Schalmont Central School District.

The District 7 schoolhouse stands on Mariaville Road near the Plotterkill Reserve. The McMillan family donated the land for the building, originally constructed in 1868.

This bird's-eye view of Pattersonville was taken looking north. The Pattersonville Hotel is in the far distance. In 1865, Pattersonville was known as Van Vechten Corners, named after the wife of Congressman Donalson, the daughter of John Van Vechten, who lived on the Flats. The name remained until 1873. Seeley Patterson and his wife, Adeline Montgomery, moved from the town of Florida and owned a considerable amount of land. Patterson was a hotel operator, farmer, and grocer on the Flats and was town supervisor of Rotterdam in 1873.

William H. Patterson, son of Seeley Patterson, was the keeper of the Pattersonville Hotel. The locals affectionately called the hotel "Cinderella's Ballroom." In 1886, Pattersonville contained 15 dwellings (including the Pattersonville), 2 stores, a wagon shop, a blacksmith shop, a shoe store, a railroad depot, and a storehouse. Ray S. Jeffers was the last proprietor of the Pattersonville Hotel before it was torn down in the early 1970s.

The Rendezvous, a large hotel, once stood on this site. It was the first building on the property that later became the site of the Pattersonville Furniture Store.

This is a c. 1930 view of the gas station that was built in front of the hotel.

In this c. 1930 picture, the gas station has been modernized with the addition of an overhang to protect the gas pumps.

Next to the gas station was a candy store. This picture was taken c. 1930.

Clyde Miller pauses for a picture while painting the curb in front of the gas station.

The hotel, the gas station, and the candy store were united in 1936, and the new building became the Pattersonville Furniture Store, a company founded by Clyde Stein.

A blowout on the Erie Canal stranded the *John L. Nice*, a canal boat. Excessive rain, flooding, or anything else that put a great deal of water in the canal could cause a blowout. This boat eventually broke in half.

This is another view of the blowout, showing the *John L. Nice* straddling the culvert. Note the piles of lumber on the boat.

Simon Hermandus Vedder originally established Vedder's Ferry in 1790. Although the ferry was at first a rowboat, a flat-bottomed scow was built in 1835 so that farm wagons and, later, cars could be ferried across the Mohawk River. J. Hoffman bought the rights to the ferry c. 1835. This picture was taken c. 1915.

Ferry Street in Pattersonville can be seen across the Mohawk River. This picture was taken from the hamlet of Hoffman's.

This photograph shows a sunny afternoon on Ferry Street c. 1902. The Canal Bridge can be seen in the background.

People are canoeing on the canal near the Patterson Road Bridge No. 76 on Ferry Street. The towpath can be seen clearly in this picture.

On the left, the closest house on Old State Road has been torn down. The next three houses still stand. The old depot is on the right.

The Veeder House is located on Old River Road (Route 5S). The house has exposed ceiling beams, wide plank floors, and wide plank wainscoting. The Erie Canal was to the south.

Donald McDougall, a longtime resident of Pattersonville, points out interesting features of an old barn that once housed teams of horses and mules used on the Erie Canal. The second story held feed, grain, and lumber. The building was razed in 1963 for a housing development.

A patriotic anniversary parade and pageant were held in July 1932. The parade celebrated the 200th anniversary of George Washington's birth.

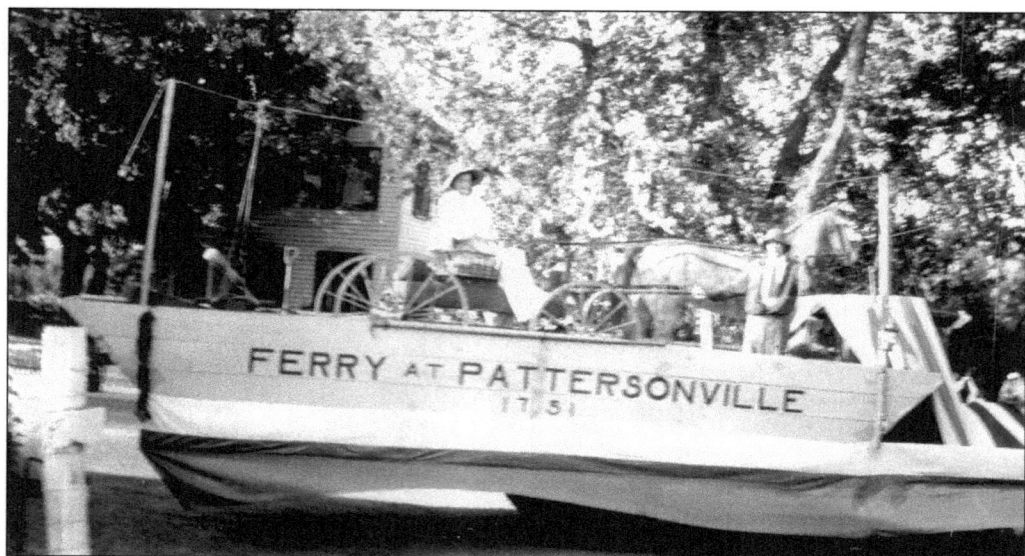

A ferry float was in the parade. The "1751" on the float may be the date when settlers first crossed the Mohawk River at Pattersonville.

In his retirement years, Reverend Hill, pastor of the Woestina Reformed Church, moved with his wife to Pattersonville.

Four

CARMAN

Looking toward Albany, this view shows the section tower at Athens Junction (Carman). The tower was located at the intersection of Chrysler and Hamburg Streets and Tower Avenue.

The railroad signal tower was also at Athens Junction (Carman).

In 1831, the Mohawk and Hudson Railroad used huge stones to support stringers on which rails were spiked.

Carman Road was a dirt road seemingly in a forest c. 1910. It was named for William Carman, who c. 1900 was a grocer and postmaster in Athens Junction. The mailbags left at the railroad station were marked for the postmaster.

New York State Thruway Exit 25, off Carman Road in Carman, is shown prior to 1958 and the building of Route 890.

The old Carman Methodist Church began services in 1898. At first, services were held in the Carman schoolhouse. In 1900, Sunday school was held in William Carman's grocery store. The church was incorporated in 1915, and its first building was erected in 1916. In 1967, the new church on the corner of Hamburg Street and Chepstow Road was consecrated. The interior is shown below.

Carman Presbyterian was a mission church of the First Presbyterian of Schenectady. Worship service began in 1946. The congregation erected a temporary building in 1954, organized as a separate church in 1955, and constructed a new edifice in 1958.

St. Gabriel's Church was founded in 1956. Mass was held in the Carman firehouse for two years. The church was completed in 1958.

The Carman Fire Department organized in 1909. It reorganized in 1933 and stored its equipment in a barn on First Street. In the late 1940s, a new firehouse was built. An addition and renovations were made in 1974.

The old fire alarm was located at the junction of Hamburg Street and Chrisler Avenue in the early 1900s.

General Electric Carman Works Building No. 1 (left) was a cloth-coating department. Building No. 2 (right) was the powerhouse.

General Electric Carman Works housed the varnish-boiling and mixing departments.

Col. Daniel David Campbell built a house *c.* 1884 for his wife, Julia, who suffered from asthma. The mansion was built with summerhouses and a half-mile racetrack. Later, Campbell gave the estate to his daughter Grace, who married Samuel R. James, and the home became known as the James Estate. Pictured on the dock is Elizabeth Clute Campbell, a family member.

On the estate were many carriage paths similar to this one so that Julia Campbell could ride in comfort. This picture dates from *c.* 1890.

After World War II, Peter Palazini and sons Raymond and Nico formed a company called Coldbrook Inc. and purchased the 200-acre Samuel James Estate, known as Coldbrook. The 200 acres lay between Altamont Avenue and Hamburg Street.

This view of the corner of Hamburg Street and Cardiff Road was taken c. 1952. Notice the new houses (Coldbrook Manor) on the right.

District 13 school was on the corner of Hamburg Street and Campbell Road, in the area known as Atherns Junction. The school's chief mentor was Herman L. Bradt, principal, eighth-grade teacher, and scoutmaster for Troop 32. The one-room school with a belfry is pictured in 1882. The Carman Senior Citizens Center is now located on this site.

Carman's baseball team is pictured c. 1910, with the Kaufman's house in the background.

Five

THE MABEE FARM

Jan Mabie House

This is a drawing of the Jan Pieterse Mabee House, purchased in 1705. The name Mabee was variously spelled Mabie and Mebie. Daniel Janse Van Antwerpen originally gained possession of the property in 1680. The house, located on the Third Flat, was likely built by Van Antwerpen.

The Mabee House, with the addition of the enclosed porch and the inn in the background, is shown here. Travelers of the Mohawk River used the inn. From left to right are Margaret Mabee, Rachael Francis Mabee, and Jacob Mabee, children of Simon Mabee. This picture dates from 1884.

This more recent view of the house shows a small building that had a fireplace, a cupboard, an upstairs room, and a cellar. This structure was probably used for the extended family.

At the beginning of the 20th century, the farm was still in the possession of the Mabee family. Among the buildings on the property were four barns and a springhouse.

The Mabee property was donated to the Schenectady County Historical Society by George Franchere in 1993. All the barns had burned or been removed. The historical society acquired a Dutch barn and had it carefully taken apart and reassembled on the Mabee property.

An English barn was also moved to the property. A blacksmith worked in the barn when the property was opened to the public. Reenactments are regularly performed, and broom making is demonstrated.

The Mabee cemetery is located on less than a quarter acre near the house. No markers were placed on the graves until 1816. Peter Mabee was the first to be buried here, and Margaret Mabee was the last to be buried here, in 1914.

Six

FAMILIES

Families were important in the development of Rotterdam, and over the years, many of the families became related by marriage. These young people seem pleased with life c. 1904. They pause for a moment to have their picture taken outside the Jones House, on Main Street in Rotterdam Junction.

Daniel Campbell was of Scotch descent and came to Schenectady at the age of 23 in 1754. He became wealthy as a fur trader and merchant. He built an imposing house, designed by Samuel Fuller, on the northeast corner of Church and Ferry Streets in Schenectady in 1762. He also owned a considerable amount of land in the county. At the beginning of the Revolution, he was an avowed Loyalist, but faced with economic ruin, he took the oath of allegiance to the new nation. He was eventually elevated to the position of judge of the Court of Common Pleas in Albany County. During the Revolution he increased his fortune by supplying the American army. He died in 1802, one of the wealthiest men in the state.

Angelica Bradt Campbell was the daughter of Arent Bradt, a survivor of the 1690 massacre, and Catherine Mabee, the daughter of Jan Pieterse Mabee. She was born in the Bradt House, which was built on Schermerhorn Road by her father in 1736. She married Daniel Campbell c. 1760 and gave birth to one son, David, who died in 1801. After her husband's death, she designated one of her niece's sons, Daniel David Campbell Schermerhorn, as her sole inheritor, provided he drop the name Schermerhorn. She died in 1812 at the age of 80.

Daniel David Campbell Schermerhorn was the son of Engeltie Bradt and Jacob S. Schermerhorn, a descendant of Symon Schermerhorn, who rode to Albany on the night of the 1690 massacre to warn residents of the attack. He dropped the name Schermerhorn by an act of the state legislature some time before Angelica Bradt Campbell's death. Because of his service in the state militia, he was known as Colonel Campbell. In 1832, he purchased the Vedder Farm, on what is now Campbell Road, and constructed a large mansion for himself and his wife, the former Julia Anne Sitterly. He built stables and a large racetrack on which he trained horses and held public competitions. After his wife became asthmatic, Campbell decided that a site away from the river would be better for her health. He bought a vast tract of land in what is now Carman and built another home with summerhouses and a half-mile racetrack, which became known as Coldbrook. Campbell died in 1891.

110

Decoration Day, May 30, 1891, was celebrated at Col. Daniel David Campbell's estate Coldbrook. From left to right are the following: (first row) Col. Samuel R. James, Grace Campbell (the Campbells' daughter), Rev. Eugene L. Toy, J. V. V. Vrooman, and Joseph Darrow, John D. Campbell (who inherited the Campbell Road estate), J. Meyers, Col. Daniel David Campbell, Julia Sitterly Campbell, and Stewart Meyers; (second row) Mrs. Samuel R. James (the Campbells' daughter), Charles Winnie, Mrs. Eugene Toy, Mrs. S. Myers Sr., Mrs. Joseph Darrow, Mrs. John E. Meyers, Dora Dillenbeck Smith, and unidentified.

This is Coldbrook, the Campbell estate in Carman. Col. Daniel Campbell gave this estate to his daughters, Sarah and Grace Campbell. After Sarah's marriage to Samuel R. James, it became known as the James Estate. Samuel James owned the largest furniture and crockery store in Schenectady, located on the corner of State and Ferry Streets. Coldbrook Estates and the Hannaford Shopping Plaza on Altamont Avenue now occupy the site.

David Campbell, the grandson of Col. Daniel David Campbell, stands next to the Campbell coach. William Ross built the coach in New York City for Angelica Bradt Campbell in 1760. David Campbell inherited the Campbell Road estate and racetrack from his father, John D. Campbell, in 1908. He raised and raced horses on the estate.

Jacob Schermerhorn built the Schermerhorn Homestead in 1757. He was a descendant of Symon Schermerhorn. This is the homestead where Daniel David Campbell Schermerhorn was born in 1803. Schermerhorn descendants owned the house until *c.* 1940.

Catherine Schermerhorn was born in 1823 and was the daughter of Marie Slater Schermerhorn, who was murdered. She married Samuel Gordon in 1839.

THE TRIAL,
AND
Life and Confessions,
OF
JOHN F. VAN PATTEN,
WHO WAS INDICTED, TRIED, AND CONVICTED OF THE
MURDER

OF
MRS. MARIA SCHERMERHORN,
(ON THE 4th OF OCTOBER LAST,)
AND SENTENCED TO BE EXECUTED ON THE
25TH FEBRUARY, 1825.

SCHENECTADY:
FROM THE PRESS OF THE MOHAWK SENTINEL.
1825.

John F. Van Patten, the first man convicted and executed for murder in Rotterdam, had a tumultuous childhood that led to depression and a mental disorder. His love affair with Josenah Fonda was interrupted by her parents' discontent. In discussing the problem with Van Patten in the fall of 1824, Fonda falsely accused her cousin of disrupting the affair. Van Patten borrowed a gun, entered the John Schermerhorn home, and shot Fonda's innocent cousin, Marie Slater Schermerhorn.

116

FOR REPRESENTATIVE IN CONGRESS

TWENTY-FIRST DISTRICT

SIMON J. SCHERMERHORN

OF SCHENECTADY.

Simon J. Schermerhorn, the son of Jacob I. Schermerhorn and Maria Vedder, was born in 1827 at the Schermerhorn Homestead. He was a descendant of Arent Samuelse Bradt and was the first cousin of Daniel David Campbell. Schermerhorn served as a member of the New York State Legislature in 1862, on the Schenectady County Board of Supervisors for three terms, and as a member of Congress in 1892. He married his cousin Helen Vedder, owned considerable acreage around what is now the General Electric Company, and raised broomcorn. He died in 1901.

The Schermerhorn Mansion was constructed by Simon J. Schermerhorn in 1857. Originally, it was a simple five-bay, center-entrance Colonial, made of brick laid in common bond. In 1889, it was "Victorianized" with the addition of the peak in the front roof, the second-story bay window, the front porch, and the brick kitchen wing in the rear. Schermerhorn was a seventh-generation descendant of Jacob Janse Schermerhorn, a prosperous merchant in Beverwyck (Albany) who accompanied Arent Van Curler to Schenectady when it was chosen as an area for settlement in 1656. Ryer Schermerhorn, son of Jacob Janse Schermerhorn, was chosen as one of the original five patentees in the Governor Dongan patent in 1684 and was the sole surviving one in 1705. Schermerhorn descendants owned the mansion until 1955.

The parlor shows the opulence of the Schermerhorn family.

John J. Schermerhorn, the brother of Simon J. Schermerhorn, was born in 1817. He married his cousin Sara Elizabeth Schermerhorn, the daughter of John J. A. Schermerhorn and niece of Col. Daniel David Campbell. He raised horses and managed the racetrack on the Campbell Estate for the colonel's son John D. Campbell.

Simon and Julia Schermerhorn celebrate their 60th wedding anniversary in 1957. They were married on November 10, 1897. Simon Schermerhorn was the son of Congressman Simon J. Schermerhorn. Julia Schermerhorn was the daughter of John D. Campbell.

Simon Mabee was born in 1805 and was the great-great-grandson of Jan Pieterse Mabee. He married Hannah Marlette and inherited the management of the Mabee Farm in 1823, when his father, Maj. Jacob C. Mabee, was run over by a wagon and killed. In 1835, Simon Mabee changed the production of the farm to the new crop of broomcorn and continued to expand the the business until his death in 1879. The farm went to his son Jacob Mabee.

Margaret Ann Mabee, the daughter of Simon Mabee, was born in 1844. After the death of her brother Jacob Mabee in 1885, the Mabee Farm was in poor financial straits because of the collapse of the broomcorn industry. The property was foreclosed upon and put up for public sale. Margaret Mabee borrowed nearly $8,000 from friends and purchased the farm and house at the auction. She leased the farmlands to the Bradt family, who lived next door, and took in tenants to pay off the loans. After 1900, she lived with her sister and brother-in-law in Rotterdam Junction and worked as a cook at the Mabee House Hotel. She died in 1914, having cleared the loans several years earlier.

Rachel Frances Mabee, the daughter of Simon Mabee, was born in 1849. When her brother Jacob inherited the Mabee Farm in 1879, he attempted to turn his sisters out of the house. Rachel Mabee began legal proceedings to prevent the eviction. The siblings came to a settlement whereby the sisters could live in part of the house and use the products of the farm for themselves but not benefit from any sales. They were responsible for all of the housework and cleaning. Shortly thereafter Rachel Mabee married George A. Scrafford. She and Scrafford built a house in the newly formed Rotterdam Junction. She died in 1922, the owner of substantial tracts of land and housing around Rotterdam Junction.

George A. Scrafford was born in Pattersonville. In 1881, he married Rachel Frances Mabee. He purchased a part of the Mabee farmlands from Jacob Mabee and built the Mabee House Hotel shortly before the Rotterdam Junction rail yards were constructed in 1884. With the help of his wife, who managed the financial affairs, he also operated a store and coal company and built a number of rental houses in the fast-growing community of Rotterdam Junction. He died in 1922, just six weeks after the death of his wife.

George Scrafford, at the wheel of his car, is ready to join the parade for the opening of the Western Gateway Bridge in 1916. In the background is the Scrafford House. George Scrafford was the head of the Independent Order of Odd Fellows and the grand master of the Knights Templar in Rotterdam Junction. He was a well-liked, active member of the community, and his favorite pastime was sitting on the porch of his hotel, smoking a cigar, and talking to everyone who passed by.

The seven sons of John and Maggie (Vrooman) Putman are pictured here. John Putman lived on the road leading to Princetown, on the corner where the Fort Hunter Road crosses. His parents, Aaron and Elizabeth (Spinster) Putman, were among the first settlers of Rotterdam. From left to right are the following: (first row) John Putman, Ernestus Putman, Aaron Putman, and Henry Vrooman Putman; (second row) Oliver Putman (husband of Catherine Mabee), Sebastian Putman, and Andrew Putman (husband of Eve Angelica Mabee). Catherine and Eve Mabee were daughters of Simon Mabee.

ACKNOWLEDGMENTS

The volunteers of the Grems Doolittle Library of the Schenectady County Historical Society would like to acknowledge the following people who contributed to this book. Edward Gifford, Scott Haefner, Mildred Kruger, Kim Mabee, William Massoth, Irma Mastrean, Ann Ross, Betty Vrooman, and Mr. and Mrs. Milton Welsh contributed photographs and oral histories. Dick Whalan, Rotterdam town historian, opened his extensive collection of pictures for our use. He also researched the answers to many of our questions. The board of the Schenectady County Historical Society was supportive throughout our endeavor. The society's large photograph collection proved to be a great help in this project. Virginia Bolen, librarian at the Grems Doolittle, corresponded with Arcadia Publishing and helped edit. Jim Eignor was our chief scanner and was patient with our last-minute changes. The project would not have proceeded without the help of the following volunteers: Ann Eignor, Scott Haefner (site manager at Fort Johnson), Ann Hicks, Carol Lewis, Mary Lieber, Beth Pfaffenbach (chief editor and organizer), Ann Ross, and Cindy Seacord.

www.ingramcontent.com/pod-product-compliance
Lightning Source LLC
Chambersburg PA
CBHW050547110426
42813CB00008B/2279